A GIFT FOR:

_____

FROM

_____

Outrageous Love

A Love that *Seeks* No Reward

SHEILA WALSH

J. COUNTRYMAN
NASHVILLE, TENNESSEE

Published by the J. Countryman division of the Thomas Nelson Book Group,
Nashville, Tennessee 37214.

Published in association with Yates & Yates, LLC, attorneys and counselors,
Orange, California.

www.thomasnelson.com
www.jcountryman.com

www.womenoffaith.com

Project editor: Kathy Baker
Design: Chris Gilbert, UDG|DesignWorks, Sisters, Oregon

ISBN: 1-4041-0110-1

Printed and bound in the United States of America

DEDICATION

This book is dedicated with love to my mother, ELIZABETH WALSH. Your love for Jesus in the best and in the worst days of your life has inspired and challenged me.

One of God's greatest gifts to me is having you as my mother.

I love you,

Sheila

OUTRAGEOUS LOVE

But when the kindness and love of God our
Savior was shown, he saved us because of his
mercy. It was not because of good deeds we
did to be right with him. He saved us
through the washing that made us
new people through the Holy Spirit.

TITUS 3:4–5

1

THE OUTRAGEOUS
GIFT OF LOVE

Outrageous
EXTREME
SHOCKING
OFFENSIVE

Imagine that a movie was made of your life. Nothing is left out. Everything you have ever done, thought or imagined is there for all to see. The indiscretions of youth, the poor choices in relationships, words spoken in anger, the secret habits that are so hard to run from and so shaming in the daylight are exposed for anyone who wants to take a look.

How would you feel?

Would you want to run and hide?

If you knew that everyone in your circle had seen your movie would you still show up for dinner?

If conversation stopped when you entered the room would you turn and leave, humiliated by their silence?

And yet deep with in all of us is a desire to be known. To be known and to be loved.

How long have you ached to find a place where everything about you is known and accepted? But that's the terror right there, isn't it. "If everything about me is known how can I be accepted? If my movie was shown to those I love and whose respect I treasure, surely they would think less of me."

This is not a new dilemma. Remember Adam and Eve? One bite of that infamous apple from the tree of the knowledge of good and evil and their first, knee–jerk reaction was to hide. We have followed in their footsteps and have been hiding ever since.

Trace a path through the Old Testament, and time after time you will see the discrepancy between the Law of God and the behavior of his people. Those who loved God had their list of things to do to show that they were in relationship with him. The Levitical law gave two lists, 365 things to do and 248 things to avoid. People tried and failed, tried and failed again. The path of human failure takes us all the way from the Garden of Eden to the foot of Calvary. The path was supposed to stop there.

"But he took our suffering on him and felt our pain for us. We saw his suffering and thought God was punishing him. But he was wounded for the wrong we did; he was crushed for the evil we did. The punishment, which made us well, was given to him, and we are healed because of his wounds."

ISAIAH 53:4–5

From that dreadful slaughter on the cross, where the Lamb of God took on himself the wrath of God, the path was covered over in his blood.

But wait a moment. Take a closer look. There is a path leading away from Calvary.

Is it a new path?

No. It's as old as Eden.

Even as we come to God through Christ accepting that there is no good thing in us, we then begin down the relentless path of attempting to prove to God that he made a good choice when he accepted us. The old laws were left at the foot of the cross, but we took up our pens and came up with new ones.

We all have our lists. We carry internally the things that we know we should do as a good wife, a good mom, a daughter, a sister, a friend, a faithful follower of Christ. We know we miss the mark too often. Our husbands or children bear the brunt of a frayed day. Those we work with can come under the barrage of words that pour out before we are able to stop them.

But there is another list. It's a longer list. It is a list that we keep inside ourselves. Secret thoughts and desires, resentment and unspoken words that gain strength in the silence of our souls. We want to be women of integrity and kindness. We want to be gentle and slow to speak in anger, but it seems as if we are pulled between our ideal self and who we really are. So once more, just as Adam and Eve did before us, we learn to hide. As we put on our clothes in the morning we learn to cloak our true self as well. We smile and say that we are fine even when it seems to us that we are dying inside. We sit through one more Bible study longing to say, "This is not working for me in my life right now," but we keep quiet. We don't want to rock the boat or be different or seem as if we have no faith.

We have traveled a punishing path.

Will we pass this legacy on to our children too?

I became a mother for the first and only time as I turned forty years old. Several things were immediately clear.

I should have slept more the first forty years!

I adored this darling child.

I did not want to set his feet on the path of trying to be good enough for God.

I wanted him to know that on his best days and on his worst days God's love remains constant, an immovable reality in his life.

It also became clear to me that my son is a sinner. So what was I to say to him? How do you explain grace and love to a child and not let it appear to be a get-out-of-jail-free for life ticket?

That's the rub. In Christ we have that pass. But must the acceptance of this gift give birth to rebellion?

I don't think so.

I think when we know we are absolutely loved at all times we live out of a desire to please and honor the one we are in relationship with.

It is only when we hide that we are living in rebellion.

Perhaps not the kind of rebellion that kicks up its heels at authority, but rebellion against the glorious gift of the outrageous love of God.

"That's easy for you to say, you haven't seen my movie," you tell me. "You have no idea the shame I hide. The abortion, the affair, the lies, the secret places I hide."

That's true and yet wonderfully irrelevant. Here comes the greatest news of all!

HERE IS THE TRUTH ABOUT THE OUTRAGEOUS LOVE OF GOD:

He has seen your movie and he loves you! He knows it all. He knows more than you are willing to face in your own internal court. God knows all that is true about you—past, present and future—and he is crazy about you. You don't believe me? Does it sound too good to be true?

"LORD, you have examined me and know all about me. You know when I sit down and when I get up. You know my thoughts before I think them. You know where I go and where I lie down. You know thoroughly everything I do. LORD, even before I say a word, you already know it. You are all around me—in front and in back—and have put your hand on me. Your knowledge is amazing to me; it is more than I can understand."

PSALM 139:1–6

Have you longed for a place where you come as you are and are welcomed every time? There is such a place. Welcome to the mane of the Lion of Judah where all God's children can bury their faces when they are sad, celebrate when they are glad, rest when they are tired, and find fresh vision and purpose when they are ready to live again.

You love me again today, Lord?
Where do you find this love?
Is there no depth to the well that is you?
There is no depth to the well of need that is me.
So I come again and again and again and again
Fresh water pours over me, washes me, and restores
the battered places.
Battered by the choices I have made
And the roles that I have played
I worship you
Fount of never ending love
God of this outrageous love
I worship you

Welcome to the
outrageous love of God!

*A child has been born to us; God has
given a son to us. He will be responsible for leading
the people. His name will be
Wonderful Counselor, Powerful God, Father Who
Lives Forever, Prince of Peace. Power
and peace will be in his kingdom and will
continue to grow forever. He will rule as king on
David's throne and over David's kingdom.
He will make it strong by ruling with justice and
goodness from now on and forever.
The* LORD *All–Powerful will
do this because of his strong love for his people.*

ISAIAH 9:6–7

Two

LOVE IN
DISGUISE

Little children, wake and listen—
songs are breaking o'er the earth
While the stars in heaven glisten,
hear the news of Jesus' birth
Long ago to lonely meadows
angels brought the message down
Still each year through midnight shadows
it is heard in every town.

A STEP BACK IN TIME

There was a world between heaven and earth, such a cavern. It was a vast wasteland that stood between the outrageous love of God and the aching need of every man, woman, and child who would ever walk this earth. Try as we would, we would never be able to reach up and touch the face of God for ourselves. We stood on one side of a locked door with no key, and yet the aching knowledge that everything we have ever longed for lay on the other side. We were lost. Like Adam and Eve turned out of the Garden, we wandered.

Who could cross this place?

Who could reach us?

Who could hold on to all that is holy and pure and hold on to us as well?

The Jews knew the answer—Messiah.

"The Lord himself will give you a sign: The virgin will be pregnant. She will have a son, and she will name him Immanuel."

ISAIAH 7:14

Immanuel, God with us.

This would be an answer to a world of prayers, *God with us.*

God's people watched and waited. Even the Samaritans watched and waited.

Do you remember the woman who Jesus encountered at the well one noontime? His friends had gone into the village to find food, and Jesus was alone until she appeared. He asked her for water. She wanted to know why he, a man, a Jewish man at that, would talk to a Samaritan woman. He told her that if she knew to whom she was talking she would request water from him. As far as she could tell Jesus was speaking in riddles. He had nothing to draw water with, and if he had, why would he be asking her? She assumed that like many men before him, he was toying with her.

Jesus was not playing games. He was about to invade her world of games and lies and illusions and change everything. He told her the water he spoke of quenched a deeper thirst, a thirst that was eroding her life day by day, relationship by relationship. As he pulled back the veil on her life she recoiled at the disclosure and moved to safer territory—a theological discussion of the correct place to worship.

Theological discussions are a great place to hide from an encounter with the living God.

Jesus sliced through her discomfort and told her that worship would no longer be defined by four walls and a roof. The time was coming when worship would be in spirit and in truth.

In spirit and in truth! What a gift of heaven to the harsh realities of earth. A time was coming when we would be able to encounter God by holding on to what we believe even though we cannot yet see. We could come as we are.

Arrested by Jesus' insight the woman said,

"I know that the Messiah is coming." (Messiah is the One called Christ.) "When the Messiah comes, he will explain everything to us" (John 4:25).

They all waited for Messiah. The Jews watched and waited. The Samaritans watched and waited, the sons of Isaac and the sons of Ishmael. They all waited for an explanation for all the things that made no sense.

Why did my child die?

Why did my husband leave?

Where is their justice in this world?

Some held on still to the words of Moses to their forefathers and waited for the Prophet.

> *"The LORD your God will give you a prophet like me, who is one of your own people. Listen to him."*

DEUTERONOMY 18:15

A prophet like Moses! That's what they longed for. Not only did Moses lead God's people out of slavery in Egypt to a promised land, but their enemies were punished, too. It wasn't enough to be free. Someone should pay for what had been done to them. Justice included vengeance.

Either way, one thing was clear, God was going to send a deliverer to save his people and make sense out of the senselessness of much of life. He would bring justice, and as we all know, that means that he will get those who've hurt us. He will march into the playground of our lives and take care of the bullies once and for all.

They waited.

They watched.

Any day now he would appear.

They had no idea, however, that he would come in disguise.

A MIRACLE IN DISGUISE

The town is full of ragged faces
Hustling through the noisy streets
People pushing, children crying,
Looking for a place to sleep
They pour into Jerusalem,
Like waves upon the shore
Returning to the place of ancients
Hurry through God's door!

Will this be a night of vengeance?
Will this be Messiah's time?
Will God send this Man of Sorrows?
Liberate his children's line?
Eyes are turned upon the temple
Where the promise will appear
Hearts cry out—"God, do you hear us?
Come in power, dispel our fear."

But hush a moment, listen softly
Angel wings brush through the night
Hear them thunder 'cross the hillside
See a bold and fearless light
In a place not made for singing
To a mother's listening ear
God looks up with tender mercy
"All is well now, I am here."

What a shock!
How outrageous!

God could have shown us how great he is. He could have displayed how powerful and above us he is. Instead he became as small as we are. He could have roared on top of a mountain, but he whispered in the voice of a baby. He could have ordered our obedience; instead he calls for our hearts.

No one was waiting for a Savior in diapers.

No one was looking at a teenage girl to spill their deliverer out onto straw and hay.

They missed the miracle.

It is outrageous for the Christ whose rightful place is at the right hand of the Father to step out of timelessness into say . . . Tuesday evening, to exchange the worship of angels for the garb of a carpenter who wore perhaps . . . size eleven sandals.

No wonder they missed the miracle. It was so close to them they almost tripped over it.

ANOTHER
CHRISTMAS MORNING

I just wanted one thing. One thing, that was all.

I wanted a baby doll. I didn't care if my sister, Frances, had a boatload of gifts. I would celebrate with my brother, Stephen, if his presents stretched from Glasgow to Edinburgh. I just wanted this one thing.

I wanted a baby doll.

Every Christmas morning was the same in our small home on the west coast of Scotland. Stephen and I would wake Mom and be sent back to bed as it was only five o'clock in the morning. We'd wake her again at six and finally persuade her to let us investigate by seven.

I will never forget that morning. I let Frances and Stephen go ahead of me. Even as I walked into the living room I didn't look at my chair first.

What if she wasn't there? What would I do?

I saw that Stephen had his robot that performed twenty-five different actions.

I saw Frances had a pile of books that would keep her engrossed and anti-social for months.

Finally I looked at my gifts. After a quick scan I began to panic.

I couldn't see her anywhere.

Mom asked me if I was going to open my presents. I smiled a feeble smile and began to peel Christmas paper off an assortment of toys and games piled high on the chair that was mine. There were puzzles and games and candy but she wasn't there.

There was no baby doll.

For me, the manger was empty.

Then my mother said, "Aren't you going to open your other gift?"

"What other gift?" I asked.

"The one at your feet," she said, laughing.

I looked down and there she was, lying in a little cradle. I'd been so close to her I'd missed her altogether. I'd been so busy looking up at the gifts in the chair that I missed the one at my feet.

> *And God the Father took his heart*
> *And laid him at our feet*
> *A tiny baby placed into our hands*
> *And heaven rang as angels sang*
> *Peace to all the earth*

Where are you looking for God today?

His outrageous love brought him right to your door, straight to your heart.

Don't look out there.
He is here!

But God's mercy is great, and he loved us
very much. Though we were
spiritually dead because of the things we did
against God, he gave us new life with Christ.
You have been saved by God's grace.

EPHESIANS 2:4–5

3

THE EYES
OF LOVE

"Well that doesn't seem fair!" my indignant son protested loudly.

"Why is it not fair?" I asked

"I didn't get to go to the party. I didn't get any cake or ice cream or anything, but I still give him a gift?"

"That's right," I said. "The point is that we are celebrating his birthday, not one more opportunity for you to lose all reason in a sugar–induced haze."

"But he's been mean to me, Mom."

My son is a generous boy. He usually likes to share and he has a tender heart, but he was stumped by this dilemma. Fifteen boys were invited to the party. Fourteen were able to go and join in the celebration with all the fun and furor that entailed, but the fifteenth, my son, did not because we were out of town. Add indignity to indignity he still was being asked by his mother to take a gift to school on Monday and to a boy who had been mean to him.

"Should we call him and tell him the gift's on the way in case he wants to bring my cake and ice cream to school?" he asked.

"Probably not," I said.

"Should I ask him if he's sorry for being mean before I give him the gift?"

"Probably not," I repeated. I was no help at all.

That night as we sat around the dinner table I asked him how his gift–giving episode went.

"It was good, Mom. You were right. He's my friend again and he liked the present. He told me that he didn't expect me to give him one because he'd been mean to me. I told him I didn't expect to either but he loved it. He had a big smile on his face."

He carried his clean plate over to the sink.

"By the way," I added. "I think this is for you."

He looked up and his eyes filled with boyish wonder as he saw the huge piece of cake dripping with ice cream that I held out to him.

"Did you make this for me, Mom?" he asked.

"I did."

"Did you do it because I had such a good attitude?"

"No," I replied, stifling my laughter. "I did it because I love you."

THROUGH GOD'S EYES

God's love doesn't play by the rules. It is not reasonable. It offers the same grace and mercy to the one who appears to have everything and the one who appears to have nothing. It offers unconditional love to the one who knows she is guilty and the one who thinks she is innocent.

This is a great surprise to both.

They said to Jesus, "Teacher, this woman was caught having sexual relations with a man who is not her husband. The Law of Moses commands that we stone to death every woman who does this. What do you say we should do?" They were asking this to trick Jesus so that they could have some charge against him. But Jesus bent over and started writing on the ground with his finger. When they continued to ask Jesus their question, he rose up and said, "Anyone here who has never sinned can throw the first stone at her." Then Jesus bent over again and wrote on the ground. Those who heard Jesus began to leave one by one, first the older men and then the others. Jesus was left there alone with the woman standing before him.

JOHN 8:4–9

What did she think as she was being dragged through the streets that day? She knew that one way or another her life was over. Soon everyone in town would know for sure what some had always thought—she was that kind of woman. She would have to leave town, if she survived the nightmare at all. She couldn't stay there. Hatred kills you slowly like a cruel disease invading your body cell by cell.

Where were they taking her? She kept her head down. Tears blinded her. She stumbled as strong arms that offered no comfort pulled her forward. Suddenly they stopped. She couldn't look up. She heard voices inflamed with accusation. Someone cruelly pinched her skin as she was left to stand in front of the crowd alone.

"I won't look up," she thought. "They can kill me if they want to, but I will not look into their eyes again." Their hatred had burned into her soul like a virulent acid. "What else can they do to me now, for surely I am as good as dead inside."

Voices. She heard voices crying out, indicting her. They spoke so loudly that she wanted to scream and scream until she was louder than all of them, but she said nothing. A new voice. A different voice spoke. He askcd a question. Was he talking to her? She didn't think so. She waited, waited for the stones to hit her body. "I wish I was dead," she thought. "Just be quick." She heard footsteps walk away from her. Where was everyone going? The courtyard became quiet, too quiet. Dare she look up? That voice. She heard that voice again. This time he was talking to her.

"Where are they?" he asked. "Where are your accusers? Did no one judge you guilty?"

Slowly she raised her head. They were gone. They were all gone. Only one man remained. She looked at him, and the tidal wave of the love of God that poured from his eyes to her broken heart almost knocked her off her feet.

"No, sir," she whispered.

"Neither do I. Go and live differently."

Years later did she sit with a granddaughter on her lap, tears pouring down the little girl's face?

"No one likes me, Grandma. No one wants to play with me. I must be ugly.

"That's just not possible, my sweet girl. You are beautiful!"

She spoke with the authority of one who had looked into the face of God at the worst moment of her life and saw his smile.

My Prison

I looked at my reflection in the mirror. It was hard to reconcile this image with the date on my birth certificate. I looked so old. I was thirty–six but I looked much older. For weeks I hadn't slept or eaten well. I had dropped fifteen pounds, a significant amount on a five feet four inch frame. They had taken my makeup away last night when I checked in.

"Why do you want my makeup?" I asked.

"We take away anything you could hurt yourself or someone else with," the nurse replied softly.

"Death by lipstick?" I asked.

She smiled and took it anyway.

I thought about the way that I had used makeup to hide from the world. If I didn't sleep I just used more concealer. If I was pale I used more foundation or blusher. Anything to avoid the questions.

"Are you all right?"

"Is there something wrong?"

As far as I could tell, everything was wrong.

How could someone who loved God be clinically depressed? How could a Christian leader end up in a psychiatric hospital? Why was I so sad all the time?

I looked at my face, stripped of all its secret weapons. There was no avoiding the questions now. These were the questions that poured from my own heart.

God, do you see me here?
Are you with me here?
I am frightened and alone.
God, can you love me here?
Can you reach me here?
I'm a million miles from home.

DIARY—OCTOBER 1992

In 1992 I entered a prison to be set free. Even as I type these words I see so clearly now that God often takes us to the place of our greatest imprisonment to bring us his greatest deliverance.

I spent one month in that hospital.

One month began to change my life and set me on a new path.

One month gave me a new compass for my journey.

One month gave me a place and time to stop running and let God love me.

I wanted to be perfect, but in the place of my greatest imperfection I began to see through different eyes. I had tried for years to dress up the outer shell of my life, but when it crumbled I could not escape that quiet voice in my heart.

I love you
I love you
I love you
I see you as you are and I love you
I always have
I always will

So I responded.

Nothing in my hands I bring
Simply to thy cross I cling

I had nothing in common with the woman dragged before Jesus, and yet I had everything in common with her. We were lost, exposed, accused either externally or internally, and alone. Neither of us expected what we saw when we looked into the face of God. We both expected judgment and received mercy.

Perhaps if you stop for a moment you might hear this voice.

Perhaps if you look up you, too, will be bowled over by a tidal wave of outrageous love if you will just let go of who you see yourself to be. Take another look through the eyes of God's outrageous love.

All to Jesus I surrender,
Lord, I give myself to Thee;
Fill me with Thy love and power,
Let Thy blessing fall on me.

I surrender all,
I surrender all,
All to Thee,
My blessed Savior,
I surrender all.

JUDSON W. VAN DE VENTER

But when the chief priests and scribes saw the
wonderful things that he did, and the children crying
out in the temple and saying, "Hosanna to the Son
of David!" they were indignant and said
to him, "Do you hear what these are saying?"

And Jesus said to them, "Yes. Have you never read,
'Out of the mouth of babes and nursing infants
You have perfected praise.'"

MATTHEW 21:15

4

OFFENDED
BY LOVE

God's love is outrageous!

It always has been—always will be. It's offensive to many for it excludes no one who will receive it.

Let's revisit that early morning miracle in the temple courtyard and take a look at who else was there that day. Not everyone walked away bathed in grace. The main players in this drama were extremely offended.

It was an unusual morning in many ways. Jerusalem was already busy even though it was just past dawn. The Feast of Tabernacles had finished the previous evening, and many visitors would still be milling around before returning to their villages and homes. Seeing Jesus sitting in the temple courtyard was an invitation to listen in. This is how all rabbis taught. It was the position of authority, and so a crowd gathered around him. Suddenly, a group of Scribes and Pharisees burst into this respected environment, dragging with them a woman caught in the sin of adultery. The agenda was to use her situation to trap Christ. They gave Jesus two choices.

Would he uphold Jewish law?
Would he uphold Roman law?

Jewish law said she should be stoned, but Roman law said Jews were not allowed to carry out their own executions. Remember when Pilate tried to move the guilt of crucifying Jesus from his court to the Jewish forum?

Then Pilate said to them, "You take Him and judge Him according to your law." Therefore the Jews said to him, "It is not lawful for us to put anyone to death" (John 18:31, NKJV).

Whichever side Jesus came down on, the Scribes and Pharisees would consider it a win. They had him trapped. The woman was a pawn, a guilty pawn but still a means to a greater end for these religious leaders.

"So what should we do, Jesus?"

"Tell us what to do, wise one?"

"Speak now and put a noose around your own neck."

Silence.

Everyone waited to hear what Jesus would say. The woman's heart must have been beating wildly in her chest as she stood at the mercy of this savage crowd. Jesus ignored their urgency and began to write in the sand.

They grew impatient and asked him again.

"But Jesus bent over and started writing on the ground with his finger. When they continued to ask Jesus their question, he raised up and said, 'Anyone here who has never sinned can throw the first stone at her'" (John 8:6–7).

Stunned silence.

They began to walk away. The text tells us that from the eldest to the youngest they left. Why in that order? Was it because those who had lived longer had a more substantial list of internal offenses, or was it because they were instantly more offended by the very idea of being compared to such a woman?

One by one they left the temple courtyard until only two figures remained. One held within her all that was wrong in the world, and one held within him all that is right in heaven, all that is true about God's outrageous love. One lived in a prison of darkness and one was The Light.

It was a miracle and an extreme affront.

It was a miracle for the woman caught in the act of adultery. She expected a stoning, if not physical, certainly verbal as the cold hard rocks of religious condemnation battered against her heart. Instead she had an encounter with the Lamb of God. No rocks were thrown that morning, just oil, the oil of peace and grace poured over a sinner's fractured life.

But there's more going on here. It is an affront to those who walked away. Take a look at the crowd. They are furious! Rage boils in their blood as the full implication of what Jesus has just said hits them.

"How dare he talk to us like that!"

"How dare he put us in the same category as that woman!"

"Did he hear what she has done?"

"Does he know who we are?"

Those who accused her were the teachers of the law. They were the ones who upheld moral righteousness. They were the ones the community looked to for spiritual input and council, and Jesus was putting them in the same category as a woman caught in an adulterous act. Shocking! Disgraceful! What was wrong with his scales? Surely he could not think that any of their minor sins weighed the same as flagrantly flying in the face of one of the Ten Commandments? She had chosen to sin. They lived their lives committed to a staunch keeping of the laws of God. Some took the command about not looking at a woman with lust so seriously that they refused to look up at all when they were in public, thus earning the title "Bleeding Pharisees" as they continually walked into walls and other obstacles!

Now Jesus was putting them in the same boat as a woman who had followed the desires of her heart or her flesh and fly in the face of God!

Frankly, I sympathize with them. It's easy to dismiss or categorize the Scribes and Pharisees because we live this side of Calvary. We have the New Testament. We are able to read how Jesus addressed them and shined his light on their hypocrisy. But on that morning all they had was the Old Testament law. That was the revealed law of God. They lived within those walls. Those walls were their homes. Jesus stepped into that arena and began to tear down all the walls. It's tough to wrestle with the way that God in Christ invaded our world and turned everything upside down. Being good was no longer enough. Following the rules wasn't going to cut it anymore. Jesus wanted so much more. It's hard to know where you stand with that kind of love.

"But I say to you who hear: Love your enemies, do good to those who hate you, bless those who curse you, and pray for those who spitefully use you. To him who strikes you on the one cheek, offer the other also. And from him who takes away your cloak, do not withhold your tunic either. Give to everyone who asks of you. And from him who takes away your goods do not ask them back. And just as you want men to do to you, you also do to them likewise."

LUKE 6:27–31 (NKJV)

That's just not reasonable, it's not sensible, it's not in us, it's not human. It doesn't sound right.

Do good to those who hate you?

Bless those who curse you?

If someone takes your coat, give him your shirt too?

That kind of behavior could lead to chaos.

Not Safe, but Good

Have you ever read C. S. Lewis's classic book *The Lion, The Witch and the Wardrobe?* It's a wonderful book full of wisdom and insight for young and old. Four children are evacuated from London to the English countryside during World War II. Lucy, the youngest child, discovers the magical world of Narnia that's accessible through a wardrobe in a spare room. At first her brothers and sister refuse to believe there is such a place until they, too, pass through the wardrobe to the world hidden behind a rack of fur coats. There they find the wicked Snow Queen and the magnificent Aslan. In this tale, the lion Aslan represents Christ. The children are overwhelmed by this majestic animal and want to know if he is safe.

"Oh no," they are told. "He is not safe, but he is good!"

That's just it though; God's not safe in the sense that we have him in a box, predictable and measured. We don't get to control how God operates. No magical formula assures the way God works. Just when we think we have a handle on his ways, God does something we never expected. He will not live in a man–made box. That would be so much easier.

Dear God,
My life would be much easier if I had you in a box
If I could have a list to keep of things to do before I sleep
And things to do throughout each day to guarantee you'd act one way
To keep my children safe and strong
Protect my family from harm
I'd keep a thousand rules each day if only that would make you say
"You've earned my favor, passed the test
Now life will be as you have asked"
Please help me, God, to understand
This life, this strange outrageous plan.

We Want Justice

God's outrageous, offensive love demands a response. We either bow to His majesty or we plot for His demise. As the Scribes and Pharisees left that day it became clear to them that something had to be done about this man if they were to preserve their power. Christ was splashing color onto their neat and ordered, black and white world.

The Old Testament law was clearly black and white. That was easy to understand. You know where you are with those two colors. Good people feel safe and those who choose to harm others know what's coming to them. They've been warned.

> *"But if any harm follows, then you shall give life for life, eye for eye, tooth for tooth, hand for hand, foot for foot, burn for burn, wound for wound, stripe for stripe."*
>
> EXODUS 21:23–25 (NKJV)

Something in all of us wants life to be fair. I see it in my son.

"He took my candy so I'm taking his!"

I've seen it in myself.

"Lord, she hurt me so deeply. I hope one day she knows what that feels like, so that she will be more careful with her words."

But Jesus came to turn everything upside down.

"You have heard that it was said, 'An eye for an eye and a tooth for a tooth.' But I tell you not to resist an evil person. But whoever slaps you on your right cheek, turn the other to him also. If anyone wants to sue you and take away your tunic, let him have your cloak also. And whoever compels you to go one mile, go with him two. Give to him who asks you, and from him who wants to borrow from you do not turn away."

MATTHEW 5:38–42 (NKJV)

What could Jesus possibly mean? Are we to turn into people who let the world walk all over us, who don't defend ourselves in evil times, who allow violence free rein, who encourage others to take advantage of us?

Are we to teach our children to live like that? Or is it possible we might be missing the point here?

There are two huge issues here:

1. Our desire for revenge
2. God's big surprise

The first one addresses why we find God's love so offensive. His love asks us to surrender our desire for revenge.

Old Testament law can seem barbaric, "An eye for an eye and a tooth for a tooth." In reality it was set in place to limit revenge. It was actually a protective law for public vengeance—you can't demand more than was taken from you. If you bring that principle into our culture the outcome would be shocking. Our society is being eroded by greedy lawsuits and a maelstrom of petty litigation.

I remember a conversation I had with a member of staff when I was co-host of *The 700 Club* on the Christian Broadcasting Network. She had been involved in a small accident, a fender–bender on the way to work. I asked her if there was anything I could do to help her. Her reply shocked me.

"No, I'm great. I'm praising God for this provision. This will get me out of all my credit card debt."

"How will it do that?" I asked naively.

"I'll sue. I should get quite a bit if I can get one of those surgical collars to wear to court. This is such an answer to prayer!"

She was sincere, and I felt as if I had landed on another planet.

The Levitical law was put in place to limit human greed and corral our desire for revenge. Let me say here, I am not against someone being fairly recompensed for an injury, but it seems as if our culture encourages all that is the darkest side of our humanity. Paul addressed that issue in his letter to the church in Rome.

> *Beloved, do not avenge yourselves, but rather give place to wrath; for it is written, "Vengeance is Mine, I will repay," says the Lord.*
> *Do not be overcome by evil, but overcome evil with good.*
>
> ROMANS 12:19, 21 (NKJV)

God's law was put in place to set limits and safeguard people in a public arena. The limits remained in place until God delivered his big surprise. His surprise blew everything we knew to be true right out of the water, and even as our rules and lists lay shredded at our feet Christ presented us with the opportunity of a lifetime.

Read on!

"I came down from heaven to do what God wants me to do, not what I want to do."

JOHN 6:38

"God could have used magic words to make the nails fall off the cross but he didn't. That's love."

A FIVE-YEAR-OLD CHILD

5

No Agenda
but Love

A Conversation
in Bethany

"*What do you think it all means,*" Martha asked her husband.

"*I'm not sure I know,*" he replied.

"*There was just something about his voice,*" she continued. "*I've never heard such a strong sentence spoken so softly.*"

"*But what a statement! Who could throw a stone after that?*" Luke asked.

"*And how could they all have been witnesses?*" Martha asked.

Jewish law required the witnesses in any case of capital punishment to begin the stoning. Her accusers were the religious leaders. How could they all have witnessed this act? Such a sin usually would be a secret one, a private guilt. It's certainly possible that someone walked in on her, a husband or family member, but *all* the Scribes and Pharisees? That would be impossible, unless the whole thing was a set–up. So what were they to do? Each one of the accusers either would have to admit he was guilty of setting a trap, or admit that he did not witness the act and refrain from demanding the woman's death.

"Anyone here who has never sinned can throw the first stone at her."

JOHN 8:7

Luke and Martha had been there that morning. They were listening intently as Jesus taught when suddenly a wave of power swept through the quiet crowd demanding attention. The tension and hatred in the air had burned into Martha as she flushed with shame for the woman who stood alone. She heard what Jesus said and watched as people began to disperse. She was one of the last to leave. She wanted to know what Jesus would say to the woman. Would he condemn her? He couldn't tell her it didn't matter, not if he truly was a man from God, and yet she couldn't imagine this unusual, compassionate man condemning a woman to death. She was stuck between two choices and neither seemed to fit. She slowly followed her husband away from the courtyard to begin their journey home to Bethany.

A few days later she saw the woman again. She wasn't sure at first, but when she got closer Martha was sure it was her.

"Excuse me," Martha began. "I don't mean to pry but I was there that morning . . . in the courtyard."

"Oh, I know what morning you mean," the woman said with a tender smile.

Martha continued. "I just wondered what . . . what he said to you. He seemed more angry with your accusers than with you but . . . well, I don't know what I'm asking really."

The woman turned to face Martha, and she took her hands in her own.

"He told me he didn't accuse me," she began.

"Oh!" Martha said, pulling back a little, unable to keep the shocked tone out of her voice.

The woman squeezed her hands. "He also told me to sin no more!"

There it is! There is the great gift that Christ brought all the way from the very courts of heaven to streets of Jerusalem, Capernaum or Chicago.

I forgive you everything
Live differently

The outrageous message was not, "I forgive you, so go and live any way you want." Neither was it, "Because of how you have lived there is no forgiveness." The glorious message, God's great surprise, was that everything about us is known and can be forgiven through Christ's sacrifice—and through the power of the Holy Spirit we can live differently.

The crowd had much in common that day, and much that divided them, but everyone in the crowd apart from Christ had their own agenda.

The religious leaders had their agenda, and it was to trap and discredit Jesus.

The others in the crowd had agendas of their own. Some came out of curiosity, some because they believed that Jesus was sent from God. Some hoped for help for their lives, for healing or comfort.

Christ had one purpose and one purpose alone. His only purpose was to do the will of his Father. His only purpose was to live out his days on earth—fully human, fully divine—and be the perfect sacrifice for you and for me. He came to show us what God looks like and to show us how to love him as he loves us.

THE BIGGER PICTURE

I wonder what happened to that woman after her encounter with Christ? Did she gratefully accept his kindness, escape, and leave town to begin a new life where no one knew her or her reputation? If that's all she did, she missed the miracle by a mile. Her greatest need was not for a way out of her present situation. Her great need was for an encounter with Christ who is himself, The Way. If her path didn't change, nothing lasting really changed at all. What would you ask for?

Imagine that it's Sunday just after church. Everyone is filing out of the sanctuary. Some are heading home for lunch; others are going out to eat. Everyone is talking about the lovely service. You are scanning the crowd to locate your teenagers, anxious to get to the nursery and collect your little "surprise" before everyone else picks up their wee ones and you have to endure that certain look from the nursery worker, tardy mom!

There is an insistent tap on your shoulder. You turn around. It's the pastor.

"Margaret, will you wait for a moment,' he asks.

"Certainly, Pastor," you reply. "Let me just signal Jim to pick up Abby."

You follow the pastor to the first row of the sanctuary, just in front of the altar.

"I have some unusual news for you," he begins. "Jesus wants to meet you here this morning."

"That's lovely, Pastor," you reply, a little confused. "Jesus often meets me here."

"That's not what I mean," he says. "Jesus Christ himself wants to come in here and sit and talk with you."

"I don't understand," you say.

"He wants to talk to you. All he wants to know is what you consider to be the greatest need in your life. Whatever it is, he will meet that need today."

"Anything?" you ask.

"Anything," he replies. "But just one thing. You must identify your greatest need. You have five minutes to think about it."

"Five minutes!" you think. "My goodness."

Your mind throws up various offerings and your list grows.

I could ask for all my kids to give their lives to him today.

I could ask for Mom's cancer to be healed.

I guess I could ask for world peace, but I don't think that will happen this side of heaven.

Our finances are a bit of a mess since Abby came.

You wonder if you have time to call Jim on his cell phone but suddenly . . . you hear soft footsteps behind you. You bow your head, afraid to look up. You hear a soft voice speak your name.

"Margaret."

"Yes, Lord."

"Margaret, tell me the area of your greatest need, for it is my heart to meet that need today."

Your mind races but as you lift your head and look into his eyes your list dissipates like the morning mist.

"I want to know you more," you whisper, grasping clearly for the first time that nothing else really matters.

"Because your love is better than life, I will praise you. I will praise you as long as I live. I will lift up my hands in prayer to your name. I will be content as if I had eaten the best foods. My lips will sing, and my mouth will praise you."

PSALM 63:3–5

Put yourself there. Imagine you are invited to experience a face-to-face meeting with Jesus and the promise that he would meet what you presented as your greatest need.

What would your request be?

Would it be for healing?

Would it be for the heart of a rebellious child to be turned back to God?

Would it be for a gift or would it be for The Giver himself?

Christ is our pattern, and he had no agenda of his own. All he wanted was his Father's will even when that would cost him everything.

> *"Father, if you are willing, take this cup from me; yet not my will, but yours be done."*
>
> LUKE 22:42

As Jesus knelt in the Garden of Gethsemane he was crushed by the agony of the path that would lead out of the garden that night. When he got up for the final time he knew that his Father had said, "No," he was not willing to let the cup pass. Jesus never asked again. After the resurrection he never mentioned the cross again. He didn't talk about the pain or the betrayal.

His only agenda was love. His only agenda was to embrace the will of God.

The call of outrageous love is to abandon all personal agendas and to follow Christ with glad hearts.

"And so, dear brothers and sisters, I plead with you to give your bodies to God. Let them be a living and holy sacrifice—the kind he will accept. When you think of what he has done for you, is this too much to ask? Don't copy the behavior and customs of this world, but let God transform you into a new person by changing the way you think. Then you will know what God wants you to do, and you will know how good and pleasing and perfect his will really is."

ROMANS 12:1-2

You Choose!

In the Old Testament sacrificial system the animal was slaughtered and offered to God. The priest would place his hands on the animal and symbolically transfer the sins of the people to the animal. Christ took our place. He became the perfect sacrifice, but we have a part to play, too. We are called to be living sacrifices. Do you see the choice involved? A living sacrifice can choose to crawl back off the altar if things get too hot. To live with no agenda but Christ, to live in the gift of the outrageous love of God, means we choose every day to say, "Yes!"

It is not likely that we will receive the gift of a face-to-face encounter with Christ on this earth, so how it must thrill the heart of God when we as his children follow the path that Christ left and live with no agenda but to honor and love him.

Perhaps when we get home to heaven we will meet the woman caught in adultery and changed by the outrageous love of God in Christ and stand shoulder to shoulder with her around the throne of the Lamb.

Beneath the cross of Jesus I fain would take my stand,
The shadow of a mighty rock within a weary land;
A home within the wilderness, a rest upon the way,
From the burning of the noontide heat, and the burden
*   of the day.*
Upon that cross of Jesus mine eye at times can see
The very dying form of One Who suffered there for me;
And from my stricken heart with tears two wonders
*   I confess;*
The wonders of redeeming love and my unworthiness.
I take, O cross, thy shadow for my abiding place;
I ask no other sunshine than the sunshine of His face;
Content to let the world go by to know no gain or loss,
My sinful self my only shame, my glory all the cross.

Elizabeth C. Clephane,
published posthumously in Family Treasury,
a Scottish Presbyterian magazine, in 1872

Lord Jesus Christ,
Teach me to live as you lived. May my only
agenda be to do the will of God with a glad and
grateful heart.
Amen

I will sing of the mercies of the LORD forever; With my mouth will I make known Your faithfulness to all generations. For I have said, "Mercy shall be built up forever. Your faithfulness You shall establish in the very heavens."

PSALM 89:1–2 (NKJV)

6

ANGERED
BY LOVE

It was the first time that my six–year–old son, Christian, had ever gone to bed without saying goodnight. He was angry with me. He is a good boy, but he had been purposefully disobedient that evening. And the consequence was that he would have to miss his guitar lesson the next day. He had crossed a line and he knew it. There are very few hills that I would die on as a parent, but respect and obedience are non-negotiable fields.

After he had his bath, fresh-faced and hopeful in his pajamas, he tried to reposition himself.

"If I say 'I'm sorry' can I have my guitar lesson tomorrow?" he asked.

"No, darling. I'm glad that you are sorry, but you can't have your lesson tomorrow."

"That makes me so mad!" he said.

"I understand that but it was your choice."

"You're supposed to be my buddy!" he replied indignantly.

"I'm not your buddy. I love you much more than that. I'm your mom. I love you so much that I won't say it's okay for you behave disrespectfully."

He walked away from me and got into bed.

I looked at the blond head turned defiantly to the wall.

"I love you, Christian. I love you when you make good choices and when you make bad choices. I love you on your best days and on your worst days. I love you when you love me and when you don't. I will always love you, sweet boy."

I sat in my bedroom and cried. Loving well is so hard.

Then I thought of the times without number when I have done the same thing to God.

"God I want you to do what I want you to do!"

"God I don't like this!"

"God I thought you were my buddy!"

And God says, "I love you more than that." I love you on your good days and on your bad days. I love you when you remember who I am and when you forget. I love you when you lift your face to me and when you hide your face.

"I love you."

I love you.

Your great love reaches to the skies, your truth to the clouds.

PSALM 57:10

LORD, TAKE THESE LOAVES

In 1996 God whispered an idea for a women's conference into the ear of Steve Arterburn. The vision was to have a team of female authors and speakers travel from church to church sharing their life experiences, the hilarious and the devastating. The original team was Patsy Clairmont, Luci Swindoll, Barbara Johnson, and Marilyn Meberg. At the end of that year Thelma Wells and I joined the core team. Together we are called Women of Faith. Each year we travel to about thirty cities bringing God's message of hope, grace, peace, and love.

It soon became clear that we would have to find a different venue for our events as we had outgrown even the larger churches. So in 1997 we moved to sports arenas across the country. Over a million and a half women have attended our conference and it continues to grow.

It's very humbling to be part of something like this. It's apparent to all of us that God is in charge—we just have the joy of showing up each week and sharing our lives with other women. Our events begin on a Friday evening and run through Saturday.

Each weekend I speak on Friday night. As I stand on stage and look out at fifteen thousand to twenty thousand women, I often am overwhelmed at the need and pain represented. I hear their stories over and over as I meet with them in the line where I'm signing books.

One woman has just lost a child.
One has experienced a divorce.
One has been diagnosed with breast cancer.
One has contemplated suicide.
One is being pulled under by the cold weight of depression.

The list is endless. My constant prayer is,

Lord,
 I don't know these women, but you do.
You know the pain they bear, the questions
they have, the disappointments that eat at
their souls, and the physical and emotional
suffering they endure. Please take the loaves
and fishes of my life and feed your people.
What I bring to you is not enough, so please
do what only you can do.
 We need you, Lord.
 Amen

Angry and Disappointed

"Oh, that my grief were fully weighed, And my calamity laid with it on the scales! For then it would be heavier than the sand of the sea—Therefore my words have been rash. For the arrows of the Almighty are within me; My spirit drinks in their poison. The terrors of God are arrayed against me."

JOB 6:2–4 (NKJV)

As I have listened to thousands of stories from women across the country, their disappointment and anger falls into three categories. We are disappointed in ourselves, in others, and, in our more honest moments, we are disappointed with God.

I understand the first one very well. I have mentioned that in 1992 I spent a month in a psychiatric ward, diagnosed with severe dysthymic disorder, the clinical term for depression. During my stay the doctor prescribed medication to help me through this struggle. I was very resistant to the idea of taking any kind of medication. I had images of walking up and down the hospital corridor drooling on my bathrobe and talking to an imaginary dog! The psychiatrist patiently explained that when a person is depressed their brain chemical levels have become seriously depleted, and the medication helps restore those chemicals to normal levels. Rather than making me less of who I am, it would help me be the woman God created me to be. I finally made peace with that and did indeed experience a tangible degree of restoration. I have talked about this time very publicly. I know the shame attached to any kind of mental illness and the ignorance surrounding it. It's my passion to de–mythesize the whole subject and to bring it into God's healing light. So many women suffer needlessly when help is available.

I think most people assume my struggle is in the past, that God is using me because I am "fixed." What they don't know is that I am still taking the medication twelve years later.

At the beginning of our Women of Faith year in 2003 I became increasingly frustrated with my continuing need for this kind of help. I decided that I would just stop taking it. I determined to tell no one. I thought that I would wait until Barry made some comment about how peaceful I seemed to be these days and then tell him I had taken myself off my medication. It didn't turn out as I expected. After a week Barry asked me if I had taken my pill that day.

It was apparent to him that I had not. I was so disappointed. I didn't want to need this kind of help. I wanted to be "fixed"! Through frustrated tears I argued with God.

> *Lord, I know you could heal me.*
> *One word from you and I would be*
> *totally restored.*
> *Why Lord? Don't you see what a*
> *testimony that would be?*
> *I would tell everyone that you did it.*
> *I want to be okay.*

What image do you see when you look in the mirror? Perhaps you see someone who can't lose weight. You feel that you are weak, a failure. Perhaps you see someone who can't control her temper, who blurts out those harsh words before you are able to pull them back. Do you see someone who is a moral failure, someone who has made bad choices and is left with the scars of those?

Our culture calls to us that what we need is self–esteem, that all would be well if we just felt better about ourselves. That is a lie. We live on a broken planet. It is a disappointing place. Things were never supposed to be like this. Children were not supposed to die before their parents. Cancer was never intended to decimate more and more lives each year. Marriage was meant to heal wounds, not deepen them. Since Eden we have been disappointed with ourselves. Life on this earth is hard. So what do we do with our disappointment?

As I struggled with my medication in 2003, healing came for me in a way I didn't expect. I discovered that what I needed was not self-esteem but self-acceptance through the grace of our Lord Jesus. My heavenly Father let me rant on and on until I was exhausted, and then he let me rest in his arms. As he spoke loving words to me in my spirit I finally came to the place of being able to pray,

> *Father,*
>   *Who am I to tell you how you should heal me. I know you could touch me in a moment and I would be completely restored, but if you never do that I will daily thank you for the provision and help available in this broken world. If I am left with this internal limp so that I can recognize it in another, then I thank you for that. You are good and you are God, all the time. All the time!*
>   *Amen*

I urge you to bring whatever it is about yourself that disappoints you to the Father and let him love you as you are right now. *I am not fixed but I am redeemed.* I am redeemed by the blood of the Lamb, and that beats "fixed" any day!

Every night when I tuck Christian into bed I ask him this question,

"Which boy does Mommy love?"

He will put his hand on his cheek and reply, "This boy!"

May I suggest that every time you catch your reflection in a mirror you ask yourself this question?

"Which girl does Jesus love?"

Put your hand on your cheek and say with absolute confidence, "This girl!"

When you are able to extend grace to yourself, you are ready to extend grace to others. One of the greatest struggles that we will face on this earth is forgiving those who have wounded us. We can't do it on our own, but God's outrageous love teaches us how to forgive. It is God's gift to us to help us live in a world that is not fair. Let's turn our hearts now to those who have wounded us and ask God for the grace to extend forgiveness.

Outrageous love teaches us how to forgive.

Joseph said to them, "Do not be afraid,
for am I in the place of God? But as for you,
you meant evil against me; but God
meant it for good, in order to bring it about as
it is this day, to save many people alive.
Now therefore, do not be afraid; I will provide
for you and your little ones." And he
comforted them and spoke kindly to them.

GENESIS 50:19–21 (NKJV)

7

LOVE TEACHES US
TO FORGIVE

I looked into the big brown eyes of my son, tears about to spill onto velvet cheeks, lip quivering with indignation.

"But it's not fair, Mom!" he said.

"I know darling. You're right, it's not fair." I agreed.

"Why should I forgive him when he's not sorry?"

Christian was stuck in a quagmire of injustice.

A boy had walked up to him in the school parking lot that morning and punched him for no particular reason. A teacher saw what took place and had disciplined the boy in question. She had asked him to apologize to Christian, but the boy refused.

My son was overwhelmed and indignant. It was weighing him down.

"When will he say he's sorry?" he asked me as the tears finally spilled.

"I don't know," I said. "He might not ever say he's sorry."

"Then what will I do?" my son asked.

"Let's go for a walk," I suggested. "I want you to carry something for me."

I took a two–pound bag of flour out of the pantry and handed it to Christian as we headed out the door.

"Why do you want me to carry this?" he asked.

"I'll tell you in a little while."

"It's heavy, Mom," he said after a few moments. "Can I put it down now?"

"Not yet, just a little further."

We walked in silence until we reached the edge of the lake.

"Can I put it down now?" he asked.

"Yes, you can put it down now," I said. "How did it feel carrying the flour?"

"It was too heavy," he said. "I don't want to go for any more walks if I have to carry groceries!"

"That's what it's like when we won't forgive, Christian. It's like carrying a big weight around with you. Forgiveness is God's gift to us to help us put down things that are too heavy to carry. I hope that one day the boy who punched you says that he is sorry, but until then you can take that big weight inside you and leave it at Jesus' feet."

Forgiveness is God's gift to us to help us put down things that are too heavy to carry.

It is one thing for a child to struggle with the petty injustices of the playground, but what about the enormous assaults that many face in life?

Abuse

Adultery

Lies and deception

Hatred and injustice

The list is longer than we have space for. I find Joseph's words found in Genesis 50 remarkable. Only God could give the grace to say to those who tried to ruin your life, "You meant it for evil but God meant it for good, so don't be afraid. You are off the hook."

We can read though Joseph's story in ten or fifteen minutes. It's easy to forget that for him it was years. From the moment that he was betrayed by his brothers and sold into slavery until the moment they met again, thirteen years had passed. He had been a seventeen-year-old boy when they turned on him, but when he saw them again he was a thirty-year-old married man with two children. Those thirteen years were long, hard ones. Joseph's story stands as a powerful reminder that God works his good plan even through the evil plans of evil people.

Joseph was born in Paddan Aram, Syria, when his father, Jacob, was ninety years old. He was his father's favorite child, perhaps because he was the first child Jacob had with his beloved Rachel. This favoritism festered in the hearts of Joseph's older brothers. Jealousy that is not dealt with can rapidly degenerate to hatred.

He was just seventeen when his father sent him to see how his brothers were doing in the fields, tending his flocks. They saw it as their moment to get rid of him. They debated whether or not to kill him and finally decided to sell Joseph to a traveling band of slave traders headed for Egypt (a distance of six or seven hundred miles from Paddan Aram). They went home and told their father that a wild animal had killed his beloved son.

Joseph was sold in the slave market to one of Pharaoh's officers, an Egyptian named Potiphar. Joseph could have lost himself in despair, but he worked hard for Potiphar. He proved himself to be so intelligent and trustworthy that his master put him in charge of all the affairs of the entire household. Potiphar's wife, however, had different plans for this young man. She asked Joseph to come to bed with her, and when he refused she told her husband that Joseph had tried to rape her. It was her word against his. Joseph was thrown in prison where he remained for years.

In God's timing Pharaoh's path crossed Joseph's. The Pharaoh had two dreams that disturbed him. No one in his court could interpret them for him. His chief butler, who had been in prison with Joseph, told Pharaoh about this young man who interpreted dreams. Joseph was brought to Pharaoh, and he interpreted the ruler's troubling dreams. There would be seven years of plenty and then seven years of famine in the land. Pharaoh accepted this interpretation and immediately made Joseph head of the department of state. As prime minister, Joseph became one of the officials next in rank to the Pharaoh.

During the famine, the entire world came to Egypt to buy corn. When Joseph's brothers arrived they did not recognize him, but Joseph recognized them. How must that have felt to see them again? The tables were turned. Joseph now had the power while the brothers were helpless. Who would have blamed Joseph if he had demanded revenge? His brothers had tried to destroy him and yet he said to them, "You meant evil against me; but God meant it for good." Through Joseph the entire family was saved from destruction, and the line of God's covenant promise was preserved.

Outrageous!

Where did that grace come from? It could only come from God.

Betrayed and broken,
Heart and soul,
Words unspoken
Take their toll
Bitter sadness
Silent tears
Wounds we carry
Through the years

Who can lift this dreaded burden?
Who can set my spirit free?
Lamb of God
Whose legs were broken
Come Lord Jesus,
Carry me

JUST START

Where do you begin to let go of the terrible burden of
unforgiveness? You just start where you are right now. You
can be honest and real with God. Remember, he knows
our hearts anyway. I struggled for a long time to forgive a
friend who wounded me deeply during my initial
struggle with depression. She could not understand why
a Christian, particularly one in leadership, would take
medication. She saw it as a faithless crutch. Her questions
cut me to the core. Perhaps you have heard similar things?

> *Where is your faith?*
> *There must be sin in your life.*
> *You need to pray more!*

At a time when I desperately longed for comfort I
found none. As time passed and I began to feel stronger
again, I discovered that I had a well of anger inside me
towards this person. I asked God to help me and in time
I felt that I should call my friend and talk with her.
She refused to see me. I was so mad I could have chewed
nails! I was stuck.

What do I do now, Lord?
Forgive.
She doesn't want forgiveness!
Forgive.
She's not sorry.
Forgive.
I don't want to!
I know. Forgive anyway.
I can't.
Just start.

Love is patient and kind. Love is not jealous, it does not brag, and it is not proud. Love is not rude, is not selfish, and does not get upset with others. Love does not count up wrongs that have been done. Love is not happy with evil but is happy with the truth. Love patiently accepts all things. It always trusts, always hopes, and always remains strong.

1 CORINTHIANS 13:4–7

That's what I did. I started where I was. My first prayers were pathetic.

"Well, here I am, Lord. You've asked me to forgive, so I will, but I don't really mean it."

I kept praying. Every day I prayed for my friend. I asked God to give me his heart for her. Weeks turned to months and months to years, and I found myself praying for her with tears rolling down my face. Forgiving someone doesn't mean that what they did was okay or that you have to be in their life anymore. It's a step of faith. It's getting our will in line with the will of God and saying, "Yes" when we want to say "No!"

Are you stuck in a quagmire of unforgiveness?

Do you feel like a helpless victim?

That is a lie of the enemy. God is watching over you all the time, all the time. You are never alone.

What was done to you may have been meant for evil, but stand back and watch as the sovereign God of the universe turns it to good in your life.

How long have you carried your bag of flour around with you?

Isn't it getting heavy by now?

There is a grace–soaked place to take it.

All creatures of our God and King,
Lift up your voice and with us sing,
Alleluia! Alleluia!
Thou burning sun with golden beam,
Thou silver moon with softer gleam!
Thou rushing wind that art so strong,
Ye clouds that sail in heav'n along,
O praise Him! Alleluia!
Thou rising morn, in praise rejoice,
Ye lights of evening find a voice!
And all ye men of tender heart,
Forgiving others, take your part,
O sing ye! Alleluia!
Ye who long pain and sorrow bear,
Praise God and on Him cast your care!

FRANCIS OF ASSISI

Where can I go from Your Spirit? Or where can I flee from Your presence? If I ascend into heaven, You are there; If I make my bed in hell, behold, You are there. If I take the wings of the morning, And dwell in the uttermost parts of the sea, Even there Your hand shall lead me, And Your right hand shall hold me. If I say, "Surely the darkness shall fall on me," Even the night shall be light about me; Indeed, the darkness shall not hide from You, But the night shines as the day; The darkness and the light are both alike to You.

PSALM 139:7–12 (NKJV)

LOVE MELTS
FROZEN TEARS

THE REJECT CHINA STORE

The Reject China Store in Knightsbridge, London is tucked away in the shadow of Harrods, that most magnificent of all department stores. The plates and cups they sell didn't quite make the cut for perfection. Many of the flaws are imperceptible, but they are there. When I was a poor student in London I used to frequent the Reject China Store. One Saturday morning I bought a beautiful fine china mug. I had examined it for ages, and I decided that I had the good fortune to find the one perfect mug in the reject bin. I carried it carefully home on the train. I boiled some water, put a bag of Earl Grey tea into my mug, and filled it to the brim. Almost immediately a crack appeared at the top of the mug and raced all the way to the bottom. The heat had exposed the flaw.

That always had been my fear, not that I would buy a mug and find its flaw, but that the flaw that I knew ran through my soul would be exposed by heat or warmth. So I unconsciously made an internal commitment to keep my heart frozen, cold as winter. I knew it might happen one day. I just didn't think it would happen on national television.

GOD CALLS FOR SUMMER

I will never forget that terrible day when my walls finally came crumbling down. I was interviewing a guest on my television show, *Heart to Heart*, when an unexpected question pierced my fortress. I was used to being the one who asked the questions, but someone turned the tables on me. We were on the air, about halfway through a thirty-minute show when my guest looked at me and said, "Sheila, you sit here day after day and ask others to share their hearts. How are you doing?"

Her question was so unexpected and kind that I didn't have time to reinforce my heart or run for cover. I had been aware for a long time of a deep sadness inside, but I didn't know what was wrong with me. I had fasted and prayed. I tried to exercise and eat better, but I was losing ground every day. I had an iron grip on my emotions because I didn't want to be seen as vulnerable or weak. I was afraid to start crying because I thought if I started I would never stop. Inside my heart was a wasteland of frozen tears. Into that bleak place came an innocent, caring question, "How are you?"

I stared at her, and I could feel something happening inside of me. It was like an internal avalanche. I tried to stop it, but I could feel cracks appearing in the ice.

Before I could throw to a commercial break, tears began to melt inside of me and pour down my cheeks. I was horrified. My guest didn't know what to do. She took my hand, which only made things worse; warmth has never been snow's best friend. I cried and cried. After a couple of minutes the director threw to a commercial break, and I ran out of the studio and into my dressing room. I stayed there all day. I waited until I thought all the staff would have gone home before I opened the door and left the studio. I drove to the beach and sat at the edge of the water for a long time. I had never been so afraid in my adult life. I was losing control. I thought I was losing my mind.

> *God help me!*
> *I don't know what's wrong with me,*
> *but I am so afraid.*

Two weeks later I was admitted as a psychiatric patient. This was my greatest nightmare. I thought it would be the end of me. My dad had died in a psychiatric hospital when he was in his thirties and here I was, following in his footsteps. I was to discover, though, that at the end of me, God was waiting.

> *"The LORD is my light and my salvation; Whom shall I fear? The LORD is the strength of my life; Of whom shall I be afraid?"*
>
> PSALM 27:1 (NKJV)

In the hospital I began to deal with the pain in my past associated with my father's death. I had grown up with a deep sense of shame, not that I had done something wrong, but that at some deeper level I *was* someone wrong. The brain thrombosis had changed dad's personality. He went from being a loving, kind father to a frightening stranger. The things he had once loved became the things he despised. Dad's illness and subsequent death left me with a world of unresolved questions, but the more prevalent legacy was a sense of dread.

Bad things happen with no warning
Guard your heart—it is not shatterproof.
Keep life noisy so there is little time to think.
Never let God down; work harder and harder.

I was terrified that I would end up like my dad.

When I was growing up people would say, "You're just like your dad!"

They would mean, "You sing like your dad, you laugh like your dad, your eyes are brown like your dad's."

I would hear, "There is a crack in your soul like your dad's, and one day when the pressure gets too much you will crack from top to bottom. You can run as fast as you can, work as hard as you might, but one day it will catch up with you and there is nothing you can do about it."

My father's apparent hatred of me and subsequent death left a well of tears inside my soul that had become frozen over time. God's love is outrageous. He saw my inner terror and allowed my greatest fears to be realized. In that fall of 1992 when I was admitted into a psychiatric hospital diagnosed with severe clinical depression, I never could have imagined that this place of my undoing would be the beginning of a new life. For so long I had dreaded the moment when someone would see that I didn't belong beside all the other perfect pieces of china and drop me off in a reject bin.

I didn't know that God looks for his children
in reject bins.
I had forgotten that scars and flaws and nail prints
can be marks of love.
I had become used to living in winter
until God called for summer.

I don't know your story. I don't know what you are dealing with or not dealing with. What I do know is this, God doesn't want you to merely survive, *He wants you to live!* Every weekend I listen to stories of women who have dressed in an overcoat of shame for years. Childhood tragedy leaves such deep wounds, but they are wounds that can be healed by the outrageous love of God. Perhaps like me you are afraid to face what is going on inside of you. Someone once said to me, "When the pain of remaining the same becomes greater than the pain of change, then you will be ready to change." I had reached that place. I had no idea what would happen to me when I walked through the doors of the hospital and they locked behind me. All I knew was that I couldn't live as I had been living any more. I also believed that God loved me; I just had no idea how much.

At the lowest moment of my life God's love began to melt every frozen tear that I had carried for years. It was a healing rain.

THE HEARTACHE
THAT NO ONE SEES

I've carried it around
And I've hid it from
   the light
And I've learned how
   to smile
And pretend I'm all right
But I'm tired of all this
   running
And I'm tired of the pain
It's the wounds we deny
   that drive us insane

There is a heartache that
   no one sees
A frozen tear inside of me
I think tonight I'm going
   to set it free
Come and heal the
   heartache no one sees

I'm going to go down deep
To the place that is broken
Going to embrace it
Bring it out into the open
And bathe it in forgiveness
Bathe it in His grace
Make peace with the truth
That I couldn't face

There is a heartache that
   no one sees
A frozen tear inside of me
I think tonight I'm going
   to set it free
Come and heal the
   heartache no one sees

Take this heartache,
   take this shame
Melt these tears and let
   them fall like rain.

SHEILA WALSH, CHRIS HARRIS AND ALLEN SHAMBLIN

In the hospital I was allowed to keep my Bible. I guess it wasn't considered a weapon! I found such companionship with the Psalmist, David. It was as if he stepped out of history and wept with me as my brother. Psalm Twenty–Seven became a lifeline for me.

> *I would have lost heart, unless I had believed that I would see the goodness of the LORD in the land of the living. Wait on the LORD; be of good courage, and He shall strengthen your heart; wait, I say, on the LORD!*
>
> PSALM 27:13–14 (NKJV)

I think of my life now in two parts, my beginning and my beginning again. My beginning took thirty–five years, but my beginning again is eternal. I was saved for twenty–four of my beginning years, but I wasn't really living. I was too afraid to really live until Jesus called me back from a frozen wasteland to the warmth of his presence.

Wounded healer
Gentle teacher
Lord of all things great and small
Mind restorer
Tender warrior
Lover of my heart and soul

I invite you to the warmth of the Father's heart.

"My beloved spoke, and said to me: "Rise up, my love, my fair one, And come away. For lo, the winter is past, The rain is over and gone."

Song of Solomon 2:10–11 (NKJV)

*He will not break a crushed blade of grass
or put out even a weak flame. He will not lose hope
or give up until he brings justice to the world.*

ISAIAH 42:3

9

LOVE THAT
NEVER LETS GO

THE LOVE OF GOD

He lived in a cold, bleak prison, a place of intermittent external screams and constant internal silent wails. He thought of himself as one who would never find where he belonged on this earth. They said he was crazy and perhaps he was. He could no longer tell. This was not a place to get well; it was a place to hide, a place to put people like him. He knew that he frightened those on the outside. He had seen it in their eyes. He frightened himself at times. He wondered how old he was. He could run his hands over his face and feel the lines that ran deep into the skin around his eyes. Did that mean he was old or had he been born that way? He couldn't remember. He knew that he was becoming weak. Some days passed without him moving from his palate on the floor. Would anyone remember him when he was gone? He thought not.

What could he leave behind?

What did he know?

What could he stake his fragile life on?

What did his mind anchor itself to during the few lucid moments in any given day?

He took a pencil and wrote on the wall of his room in the asylum.

"Could we with ink the ocean fill,
And were the skies of parchment made,
Were every stalk on earth a quill,
And every man a scribe by trade,
To write the love of God above,
Would drain the ocean dry.
Nor could the scroll contain the whole,
Though stretched from sky to sky."

Do you recognize these words? They are the third stanza of that beautiful hymn "The Love of God," written in 1917 by Frederick Lehman. He based the first two verses on the words of a Jewish poem written in Aramaic in 1050 by Meir Ben Isaac Nehorai, a cantor in Worms, Germany. But the third verse stands alone as the legacy of a man who spent most of his life in an asylum. Lehman said the lines had been found penciled on the wall of the inmate's room after he had been carried to his grave.

Mr. Lehman wrote on completion of the hymn,

"The general opinion was that this inmate had written the epic in moments of sanity."

I take great comfort in this gift from such a troubled and tormented soul. What this says to me is that even in our bleakest moments when no one else can reach us,

God still can and He does. For such a man to write that there is not enough ink in this world to describe God's outrageous love brings tears to my eyes. The Lord must have been a very present and frequent guest in that cell.

I know a little of that companionship. During my stay in hospital I wrote,

> *I never knew you lived so close to the floor*
> *But every time I am broken,*
> *Bent over by this weight of grief*
> *I feel your hand on my shoulder*
> *Your tears on my neck*
> *You never tell me to pull myself together*
> *To stem the flow of tears*
> *You simply stay by my side for as long as it takes*
> *So close to the floor*

I was used to singing songs of worship to a God who sits enthroned in the heavens, and our God is certainly that. But in my worst days I discovered a God who lives very near to those who are broken, those who live close to the floor. He has promised that we will not be given more than we can bear even if at times it seems as if he has taken us very close to the edge.

Human history is a tale of joy and sorrow, heartache and gladness, of unexpected grace and unmerited suffering. I often wonder how God is able to stand back and watch the cruelty that we inflict on one another or the tragedy that occurs with no help from human hands. From the moment that Adam and Eve decided to move away from God's plan until the day when Jesus Christ returns and stands on this earth, the tapestry of our lives has been muddied by regret and injustice. We live now in very troubling times. Wars and rumors of wars fill the pages of our newspapers. Flood, famine, earthquakes and all manner of natural disasters seem to be on the rise. Cancer, AIDS, heart disease, and an onslaught of new and more potent viruses assault us every day.

I hold all of that to be true, and yet my heart is filled with gladness and hope. Sometimes we become so mired in the small pieces and petty frustrations of our days that we forget the bigger picture. We must not lose sight of the big picture:

We have a present promise and a future certainty.

A Present Promise

My son stood and stared at the gift. He was thrilled and horrified at the same time. Our dear friends Frank and Marlene had sent Christian a skateboard. Marlene had warned me that the gift was on the way, so I had already purchased enough protective gear to arm Christian against an onslaught of marauding elephants. We found a flat piece of sidewalk and he gingerly got on. After a few false starts and a couple of moderate tumbles he was starting to get the hang of it.

"This is cool, Mom. Look at me!" he yelled.

I watched him for fifteen minutes, and then I told him I was going inside to grab a cup of coffee.

"No way, Mom. I can't do this without you," he said. "It won't be any fun on my own. And if I fall what will I do if you're not there to pick me up?"

I abandoned the coffee and reclaimed my spot on the sidewalk.

Isn't that what we all want? Someone to be with us in the good moments and the bad, to cheer for us when we do well and pick us up and hold us if we fall. Christ has promised us that he will never leave us or abandon us. He won't turn away or become distracted or overworked. The same God who holds the universe in place watches over you.

A FUTURE CERTAINTY

*Now I saw a new heaven and a new earth, for the
first heaven and the first earth had passed away.
Also there was no more sea. Then I, John, saw the
holy city, New Jerusalem, coming down out of
heaven from God, prepared as a bride adorned
for her husband. And I heard a loud voice from
heaven saying, "Behold, the tabernacle of God is
with men, and He will dwell with them, and they
shall be His people. God Himself will be with them
and be their God. And God will wipe away every
tear from their eyes; there shall be no more death,
nor sorrow, nor crying. There shall be no more
pain, for the former things have passed away.*

REVELATION 21:1–4 (NKJV)

This is our absolute hope. I saw that clearly when
my mother-in-law, Eleanor, was in the final stages of
liver cancer. Even as the disease took over her body,
nothing could touch her spirit. As she was losing ground
on earth, she was gaining ground in heaven. In the last
week before she died, Barry and I took turns staying with
her through the night. One night I was sitting in bed
with her, her head resting on my shoulder. She had been
restless for hours, but I was sure she was finally asleep.
I had given her the prescribed morphine and held her
like a child until her breathing became easy. I started to

softly sing some of her favorite hymns. I sang "Great is thy Faithfulness," "A Mighty Fortress is our God," and then a favorite of mine by a fellow Scot.

> O Love that wilt not let me go,
> I rest my weary soul in thee;
> I give thee back the life I owe,
> That in thine ocean depths its flow
> May richer, fuller be.

I have loved this hymn since I was a child growing up on the west coast of Scotland. George Matheson wrote it when he was forty years old in the manse of Innelan, a small town in Argyleshire, Scotland, on the evening of the 6th of June, 1882. He said of this hymn,

"I was alone in the manse at that time. It was the night of my sister's marriage, and the rest of the family were staying overnight in Glasgow. Something happened to me, which was known only to myself, and which caused me the most severe mental suffering. The hymn was the fruit of that suffering. It was the quickest bit of work I ever did in my life. I had the impression of having it dictated to me by some inward voice rather than of working it out myself. I am quite sure that the whole work was completed in five minutes, and equally sure that it never received at my hands any retouching or correction. I have no natural gift of rhythm. All the other verses I have ever written are manufactured articles; this came like a dayspring from on high."

As I sang this hymn, Eleanor squeezed my hand. I looked down at her, and tears were rolling down her cheeks.

"That's the promise, Mom," I said. "That's your promise. Jesus will never let go of you. You will go from our arms to His."

As we have journeyed through this book together my prayer for you is a simple one.

> *I pray that even at this moment you will be filled with a new awareness of the outrageous love that God has for you.*
>
> *I pray that God will bless you and those you love and fill your heart and home with his peace.*
>
> *I pray that as you face today and all your tomorrows it will be with a renewed sense of Christ's present promise and of your glorious future certainty.*
>
> *In Jesus name,*
> *Amen*

Welcome to the

outrageous love of God !